ARGUMENTS

Other titles in this
series include:

ARGUMENTS

Published in 2019 by The School of Life
First published in the USA in 2020
70 Marchmont Street, London WC1N 1AB
Copyright © The School of Life 2019
Printed in Belgium by Graphius

A proportion of this book has appeared online at
www.theschooloflife.com/thebookoflife

The School of Life is a resource for helping us understand ourselves, for
improving our relationships, our careers and our social lives – as well as
for helping us find calm and get more out of our leisure hours. We do
this through creating films, workshops, books and gifts.
www.theschooloflife.com

ISBN 978-1-912891-11-5

10 9 8 7 6 5 4 3 2

Cover photo: Jonathan Sharp

CONTENTS

An average couple will have between thirty and fifty significant arguments a year – 'significant' meaning an encounter which departs sharply from civilised norms of dialogue, would be uncomfortable to film and show friends and might involve screaming, rolled eyes, histrionic accusations, slammed doors and liberal uses of terms like 'arsehole' and 'knobhead'.

Given the intensity of the distress that arguments cause us, we could expect modern societies to have learnt to devote a great deal of attention and resources to understanding why they happen and how we might more effectively defuse or untangle them. We might expect there to be school and university courses on how to manage arguments successfully and official targets for reducing their incidence (with news bulletins anxiously reporting that the argument index had risen 1.7 per cent in the last quarter and the opposition is demanding resignations from the richly resourced Ministry of Arguments).

But there are some strong reasons for our collective neglect. The first is that our Romantic culture sentimentally implies that there might be a necessary connection between true passion and a fiery temper. It can seem as if fighting and hurling insults might be signs not of immaturity and a woeful incapacity for self-control, but of an admirable intensity of desire and strength of commitment.

Romanticism also conspires to suggest that arguments might be part of the natural weather of relationships and could never therefore be fairly analysed through reason or dismantled with logic. Only a pedant would seek to think through an argument, as opposed to letting it run its sometimes troubling and rowdy, but ultimately always necessary, course.

At a more intimate level, it may be that we cannot quite face what arguments show us about ourselves: They present an unbearable insult to our self-love. Once the argument is over, the viciousness, self-pity and pettiness on display are repulsive to have to think about, and so we artfully pretend to ourselves and our partners that what happened last night must have been a peculiar aberration, best passed over in silence from the calmer perspective of dawn.

We are further stymied in our investigations because there is so little public evidence that a version of what occurs in our unions might unfold in everyone else's as well. Out of shame and a desire to seem normal, we collectively shield each other from the reality of relationships, and then imagine that our behaviour must be uniquely savage and childish and therefore incapable of redemption or analysis. We miss out on a chance to improve because we take ourselves to be the mad exceptions.

None of this needs to be the case. We argue badly and regularly principally because we lack an education in how to teach others who we are. Beneath the surface of almost every argument lies a forlorn attempt by two people to get the other to see, acknowledge and respond to their emotional reality and sense of justice. Beyond the invective is a longing that our partner should witness, understand and endorse some crucial element of our own experience.

The tragedy of every sorry argument is that it is constructed around a horrific mismatch between the message we so badly want to send ('I need you to love me, know me, agree with me') and the manner in which we are able to deliver it (with impatient accusations, sulks, put-downs, sarcasm, exaggerated gesticulations and forceful fuck yous).

A bad argument is a failed endeavour to communicate, which perversely renders the underlying message we seek to convey ever less visible. It is our very desperation which undermines us and ushers in the unreasonableness that prevents whatever point we lay claim to from making its way across. We argue in an ugly way because, in our times of distress, we lose access to all better methods of explaining our fears, frustrated hopes, needs, concerns, excitements and convictions. And we do so principally because we are so scared that we may have ruined our lives by being in a relationship with someone who cannot fathom the inner movements of our souls; we would do things so much better if only we cared a little less.

We don't, therefore, end up in bitter arguments because we are fundamentally brutish or resolutely demented, but because we are at once so invested and yet so incapable. It is the untutored force of our wish to communicate that impedes our steady ability to do so.

And yet, though arguments may be destructive, avoiding points of conflict isn't straightforwardly the answer either. An argument is about something, and its content needs to be faced up to eventually if a relationship is to survive. The priority is not so much to avoid points of contention as to learn to handle them in less counterproductively vindictive and more gently strategic ways. It seems we may need a lot of help in order to acquire the complex art of converting our poisonous arguments into effective and compassionate dialogues.

A BRIEF HISTORY OF ARGUMENTS

Arguing in relationships is, privately, so familiar to us that it can feel like a constant of the human condition. But there is a significant historical dimension to our propensity to fight and our style of doing so. We should investigate the history and future of arguments.

Cairo, Egypt, 1550 BC

Couples in ancient Egypt are no strangers to frustrations, but the way in which these are handled reflects assumptions that will appear standard all around the world before the modern period. Far from engaging in lengthy or passionate discussion, husbands are encouraged to shut down conflict through dogmatic command and, at points, physical force. A statute from the time recommends that a wife who disagrees with her husband should be sequestered in a pit or a large earthenware jar for a time in order to restore harmony to the household.

Athens, Greece, 415 BC
The philosopher Socrates develops a reputation for being highly unusual in his way of life, not least because he is known to have many long and often contentious discussions with his wife, Xanthippe. When asked why a wise man couldn't simply render his wife obedient through brute authority, Socrates replies that conflictual conversation with a spouse will provide a philosopher with a vital education in the arts of persuasion and dialogue. The answer sounds highly weird to its first audiences.

London, England, February 1542

Henry VIII of England and his fifth wife, Catherine Howard, are in marital difficulties. Catherine is rumoured to have been conducting an affair with a courtier who is also her private secretary – and Henry is furious. But rather than argue about this, he simply issues orders to have Catherine beheaded outside the Tower of London. From the scaffold, she makes a short speech in which she describes her punishment as 'worthy and just'.

Paris, France, October 1833

The English philosopher John Stuart Mill and the feminist author Harriet Taylor meet in a small Left Bank hotel and begin a love affair guided by a radically new set of ideas about how relationships between men and women might go. Both Mill and Taylor are committed to what becomes known as companionable love, a relationship marked by mutual respect and friendship, and to even-tempered dialogue as the way to resolve tensions. Taylor will later compliment Mill by saying that he was one of the only men she had ever met who knew how to speak to a woman as if she might be as intelligent as he was.

But however noble the sentiments, most couples do not manage to emulate Taylor and Mill's unusually dignified relationship. Indeed, the principles of modern marriage manage, paradoxically, to radically increase opportunities for protracted conflict and complex disagreement. These relationships require two people to undertake a huge range of tasks – wholly in common and with thorough mutual consent – that in the past would have been split into exclusive and discussion-free spheres. They must now jointly reach decisions on what kind of rug might be nice for the parlour, what to do on Sunday afternoon, whose parents to have Christmas with, where to send a child to school, how to serve soup and how much weight either of them might lose.

Relationships come to be guided by a Romantic vision of harmonised souls. People don't merely want the reluctant acquiescence of a partner; they want them spontaneously to respond to the world in exactly the same way as they do, to share their sense of humour, to like a novel for the same reasons, to participate enthusiastically in the intricacies of their erotic imagination, to be aligned with their economic attitudes and to agree with them about interior design and the right time to go to bed. Unsurprisingly, divorce rates begin a long and sharp rise upwards.

New York, United States, 1935
Married physicians Hannah and Abraham Stone begin

to offer relationship counselling to distressed couples who find themselves unable to communicate effectively. They condense many of their learnings into a bestselling book, *A Marriage Manual*, which, among other pieces of advice, recommends that couples learn not to utter dogmatic negative assertions about what their partner is 'really' like and stick instead to explaining how the other makes them feel. We will make much more progress by saying, for example, 'You make me feel as if I don't matter to you in any way' rather than resorting to a more global and defining, 'You are a selfish and uncaring brute.'

Messenia, Greece, August 2013

Actors Ethan Hawke and Julie Delpy star in Richard Linklater's film *Before Midnight*, a study of a couple in crisis. The film becomes famous for a twenty-minute argument scene set in a Greek hotel, one of the longest and most fiery disputes in modern cinema, during which Hawke and Delpy trade insults, shout, slam doors and seethe with awesome cold fury at one another. The fractiousness on screen displays, with rare honesty, what a great many couples around the world know only too well from their own lives. People may in theory be committed to companionable marriage and civilised dialogue, but most of them still have little idea how to enact their loftier aspirations.

Intergalactic Space Station, somewhere
near Jupiter, 2200
Couples continue to face many of the same challenges as they did in the era of arguments that began in the 19th century. They still have to make tricky joint decisions (about when to hail a rocket or to download their brain) and they still seek to convey the subtle truths of their feelings, desires, fears and needs, but they don't now

get enraged or snide, and they don't shout or slam space station doors. They feel agitation, but they deal with it via techniques of therapeutic diplomacy taught to them over long years of schooling and regularly refreshed via their embedded mind-chips. They have been taught how arguments start, how to drain them of their force, how deftly to transmit important truths and how to strive to see a situation through another's eyes. There is a good deal less desperation and a lot less swearing in our gravity-less robot-vacuumed homes.

For most of human history, couples haven't fought: One person has simply asserted their will and shut the other person down. Now we are living in a far more hopeful age that trusts in equality and dialogue. And yet we have only taken the first steps towards knowing how to handle disagreement and conflict in mature and intelligent ways. We have learnt how to hope for love in our relationships; the task ahead of us is to cope more wisely and resourcefully with the moments of hate.

S ome of the reason why we argue so much and so repetitively is that we aren't guided to spot the similarities that run through our arguments; we do not have to hand an easy typology of squabbles that could be to domestic conflict what an encyclopedia of birds is to an ornithologist.

What follows, therefore, is a description and diagnosis of twenty of the most common forms of argument that unfold between couples.

Though fights can, from the outside, look generic,

with similar displays of agitation and aggression, we should come to recognise the very distinct kinds of row in operation. Each type listed here foregrounds a particular way in which we typically fail to communicate a vital and intense truth to a partner.

By examining them in turn, we may gradually assemble an understanding of some of the obstacles we face in relationships, and greet moments of dissent with a little less surprise and rather more tolerance and humorous recognition. We will be reminded once more that love is a skill, not an emotion.

I. THE INTERMINABLE ARGUMENT

One of the hardest types of argument to unpick is the type that looks, from a distance, as though it is always new and always unique. One day the argument is about something one person said to a friend, the next it is about a family reunion; sometimes the argument centres around a stain that's appeared on the sofa, at another point it's around the government's approach to the setting of interest rates.

What is surprising to imagine is that we may, unwittingly, be having the same argument in disguise. The flashpoints of agitation may superficially seem very diverse, but they are all reconfigurations of the same basic conflictual material.

Arguments about whether to take the train or the bus, or about taking out the bins, or about the economic potential of Africa, or about a scratch on a wooden table, or about whether it's OK to be five minutes late for a dental appointment, or about what to give a friend as a wedding present, or about the difference between a serviette and a napkin may all be emerging from the repeated, frustrated attempt to transmit a single intimate truth: I feel you don't respect my intelligence.

We keep arguing because we never manage to identify and address the key issue we're actually cross about; irritability is anger that lacks self-knowledge.

Why should it be so hard to trace the origins of our rage?

At points, it's because what offends us is so humiliating in structure. It can be shameful for us to realise that the person in whom we have invested so much may not in fact desire us physically, or might not fundamentally be kind, or could be exploiting us financially or gravely impeding our professional aspirations. We come under immense internal pressure not to square up to truths that would require us to make a range of practically difficult and emotionally devastating realisations. We prefer to let our anger seep out in myriad minor conflicts over seemingly not very much rather than have to argue over the direction of our lives.

We may, furthermore, not have grown up with a sense that our dissatisfactions ever deserve expression. Our parents might have been too anxious, too vulnerable or too bullying to allow much room for our early needs. We might have become masters in the art of not complaining and of accepting what we are given as the price of survival and of the protection of those we love. But this doesn't now spare us feelings of frustration; it simply makes us incapable of giving them a voice.

We are hence doomed to keep having small or diversionary squabbles so as not to have to touch the fundamental truth at the core of our complaints: You don't show me enough physical affection; My life is harder than your life; Your family are much worse than you think they are; I'm threatened by your friends; You have the wrong approach to money.

But, naturally, in the course of not having the big discussion, we poison everything else. No day is free of the marks of the conflict that has not been had.

We should learn to have the courage of our frustrations,

and of our fears. It is always better to touch the ur-argument than for a relationship to die by a thousand squabbles. We will cease to fight so much when we can face up to, and voice, what we're really furious about.

II. THE DOMESTIC ARGUMENT

There is a kind of fight that repeatedly occurs when two lovers are convinced that what is at stake is far too petty and small to have an argument about.

No well-educated, intelligent, enlightened soul would, it is assumed, spend any time in conflictual discussion with their partner about what to do with a wet towel, where dirty socks should go, how to cut a loaf of bread or how many cotton buds to order online. These themes belong to squalid, old-fashioned lives mired in the humdrum and the mediocre. Lengthy discussion might be allowed when it comes to themes of metaphysical importance – the direction of the state, the role of the free market, the rightful place of religion – but only fools would bother to discuss when and how the fridge should be cleaned.

None of this makes conflict over domestic issues less likely. It just means that when conflict does occur, it is handled impatiently, with a certainty that it shouldn't be occurring and a determination to end it as soon as possible. Unconvinced of the legitimacy of our domestic disagreements, we end up bullying and nagging on the one side, and shirking and waving away complaints on the other. One person gives up teaching in order to insist and assert; the other gives up listening in order to abscond and evade.

Successful discussion relies on a sense that there is something profound to be processed. But in our squeamishness about the tensions of domesticity, we refuse to take our complaints seriously, and so our arguments end up scrappy, lazy and oblique.

A more fruitful course would be to recognise that the deepest themes can flow beneath so-called trivial externals. A dispute about the laundry isn't really about sheets and clothes; a heated exchange about fizzy or still water isn't really about cost. The ostensible focus of the argument (the butter, the bins, the umbrella) is a symbol. It stands for something larger and more profound, which is currently out of sight but is making its powerful presence felt in an indirect way.

We should imagine that there might be an unexpectedly large fear connected to things that agitate us domestically, and accept the initially implausible notion that what is making our exchanges vicious is that we are scared. For one person, haunted by a fear of excessive compliance, being asked to do the laundry first thing on a Saturday may symbolise a life wasted through drudgery. But to another individual who has had too much experience of disintegration, it might stand for a heroic victory over the forces of chaos. A seemingly trivial fight about washing underwear can be more accurately reframed as a poignant battle against two competing terrors.

What is regrettable is that we are rarely imaginative enough to discuss the psychological themes that stir beneath the domestic, and so we concentrate our disputatious energies on the surface points of contention instead.

We should learn not just to nag and shirk around the 'small' flashpoints, but to become forensic and generous investigators of our annoyances: to ask ourselves why we are triggered by a discussion of the shopping, what a dirty towel represents or what the symbolic meaning of crumbs on a table might be, given our emotional histories. Accessing our fears and seeing how profound and all-encompassing they can be offers us relief from the fear of pettiness; our agitation isn't surprising, because genuinely significant issues are at stake. We can come to see the domestic sphere for what it really is: a superficially trivial arena in which we meet, in disguised form, the most important themes of psychology – the tension between the longing for freedom and the fear of entrapment, the horror of constraint and the desire for protection, the risks of rigidity and the anxiety of chaos – themes that deserve all the sympathetic and intelligent discussion we can muster.

III. THE DEFENSIVE ARGUMENT

We often operate in romantic life under the mistaken view – unconsciously imported from law courts and school debating traditions – that the person who is 'right' or has the stronger case should, legitimately, 'win' an argument. But this is fundamentally to misunderstand what the point of relationships might be. It is not to defeat an opponent (there are no prizes for 'winning' other than self-satisfied loneliness) so much as to try to help each other to evolve into the best versions of ourselves.

There's a kind of argument that erupts when one partner has a largely correct insight into the problems of their partner. With a stern and gleeful tone, they may declare, 'You've been drinking too much,' 'You hogged the conversation at the party,' 'You're always boasting,' 'You don't take enough responsibility,' 'You waste too much time online' or 'You never take enough exercise'. The insight is not wrong – that is what is so tricky. The critic is correct, but they are unable to 'win' because there are no prizes in love for correctly discerning the flaws of our partners. Indeed, paradoxically, by attacking a partner with clinical energy, we reduce our chances of ever reaching the real goal: the evolution of the person we have to live with.

When we're on the receiving end of a difficult insight into our failings, what makes us bristle and deny everything isn't generally the accusation itself (we know our own flaws all too well); it's the surrounding atmosphere. We know the other is right, we just can't bear to take their criticism on board given how severely it has been delivered. We start to deny everything because we are terrified: The light of truth is shining too brightly. The fear is that if we admitted our failings, we would be crushed, shown up as worthless, required to attempt an arduous, miserable process of change without sympathy or claim on the affections of the other. That's why we insist that we do actually do enough exercise, that we have been working very hard and that we have never wasted time on any embarrassing websites.

We feel so burdened with shame and guilt already that a lover's further upbraiding feels impossible to listen to. There's too much pre-existing fragility in our psyches for us to admit to another difficult insight into what's wrong with us.

Plato once outlined an idea of what he called the 'just lie'. If a crazed person comes to us and asks, 'Where's the axe?' we are entitled to lie and say we don't know, because we understand that were we to tell them the truth, they would probably use the tool to do something horrendous to us. That is, we can reasonably tell a lie when our life is in danger. In a couple, our partner may not literally be searching for an axe when they ask us an inquisitorial question, but psychologically this is precisely how we might experience it, which makes it understandable if we say we simply don't know what they are talking about.

It may feel unfair to ask the partner to take our fears on board. But if they want to help the relationship, they will need to make it clear that they won't ever use the truth (if it is acknowledged) as a weapon.

What is so sad is how easily we (as the accused) might, if only the circumstances were more sympathetic, confess to everything. We would, in fact, love to unburden ourselves and admit to what is broken and wounded in us.

People don't change when they are gruffly told what's wrong with them; they change when they feel sufficiently supported to undertake the change they (almost always) already know is due. It isn't enough to be sometimes right in relationships; we need to be generous enough in giving out signs of love in order that our partner can admit when they are in the wrong.

IV. THE SPOILING ARGUMENT

There is a kind of argument that begins when one partner deliberately – and for no immediately obvious reason – attempts to spoil the good mood and high spirits of the other.

The cheerful partner may be baking a cake for their visiting nephew or whistling a tune while they rearrange the kitchen. They may be making plans for the weekend or discussing what fun it will be to see an old school friend again soon. Or they may be expressing unusual optimism about their professional future and financial prospects.

Despite our love for them, something about the situation may suddenly grate with us. Within a short time, we may find ourselves saying something unusually harsh or critical: We point out a flaw with their school friend (they tell very boring anecdotes, they can be pretty snobbish); we take exception to their rearrangement of the cupboards; we find fault with the cake; we bring up an aspect of their work that we know our partner finds dispiriting; we complain that they haven't properly considered the roadworks when planning the weekend. We do everything to try to induce a mood of anxiety, friction and misery.

On the surface it looks as if we're simply monsters. But if we dig a little deeper, a more understandable (though no less regrettable) picture may emerge. We are acting in this way because our partner's buoyant and breezy mood can come across as a forbidding barrier to communication. We fear that their current happiness could prevent them from knowing the shame or melancholy, worry or loneliness that presently possesses us. We are trying to shatter their spirits because we are afraid of being lonely.

We don't make this argument explicitly to ourselves, but a dark instinct in our minds experiences their upbeat mood as a warning that the uncheery parts of ourselves must now be unwelcome. And so we make a crude, wholly immature but psychologically comprehensible assumption that we will never be properly known and loved until our partner can feel as sad and frustrated as we do – a plan for the recalibration of their mood that we put into motion with malicious determination.

But, of course, that's not how things pan out. We may succeed in making our partner upset, but we almost certainly won't thereby secure the imagined benefits of their gloom. They won't, once their mood has been spoilt, emerge with any greater appetite for listening to our messages of distress or for cradling us indulgently in their consoling arms. They will just be furious.

The better move – if only we could manage it – would be to confess to, rather than act out, our impulses. We should admit to our partner that we have been seized by an ugly fear about their happiness, laughingly revealing how much we would ideally love to cause a stink and firmly pledging that we won't. We would all the while remind ourselves that every cheerful person has been sad and that the buoyant among us have by far the best chances of keeping afloat those who remain emotionally at sea.

The spoiling argument is a wholly paradoxical plea for love that leaves one party ever further from the tenderness and shared insight they crave. Knowing how to spot the phenomenon should lead us – when we are the ones cheerily baking or whistling a tune – to remember that the person attempting to ruin our mood isn't perhaps just nasty (though they are a bit of that too); they are, childishly but sincerely, worried that our happiness may come at their expense. They are, through their remorseless negativity, in a garbled and maddening way, begging us for reassurance.

V. THE PATHOLOGISING ARGUMENT

There are arguments in which one person gets so upset that they start to behave in ways that range far beyond the imagined norms of civilised conduct. They speak in a highly pitched voice, they exaggerate, they weep, they beg, their words become almost incoherent, they pull their own hair, they bite their own hand or they roll on the floor.

Unsurprisingly, it can be supremely tempting for their interlocutor to assert that this dramatic behaviour means they have evidently gone mad – and to close them down on this score. To press the point home, the unagitated partner may start to speak in a preternaturally calm way, as if addressing an unruly dog or a red-faced two-year-old. They may assert that, since the partner has grown so unreasonable, there doesn't seem to be any point in continuing the conversation – a conclusion which drives the distressed partner to further paroxysms and convulsions.

It can feel natural to propose that the person who loses their temper in the course of an argument thereby loses any claim to credibility. Whatever point they may be trying to make seems automatically to be invalidated by the fact that they are doing so while in a chaotic state. The only priority seems to be to shift attention to how utterly awful and immature they are being. It is evident: The one who is calm is good; the one who is frothing and spluttering is a cretin.

Unfortunately, both partners end up trapped in an unproductive cycle that benefits neither of them.

There's a moment when the calm one may turn and say, 'Since you are mad, there's no point in talking to you.' The awareness – in the raging lover's mind – that, as they rant and flail, they are ineluctably throwing away all possibility of being properly attended to or understood feeds their ever-mounting sense of panic. They become yet more demented and exaggerated, further undermining their credibility in the discussion. Hearing their condition diagnosed as insane by the calm one serves to reinforce a suspicion that perhaps they really are mad, which in turn weakens their capacity not to be so. They lose confidence that there might be any reasonable aspect to their distress which could (theoretically) be explained in a clear way, if only they could stop crying.

'I'm not going to listen to you any further if you keep making such a fuss,' the calm partner might go on to say, prompting ever more of precisely this 'fuss'. The frustrated one is gradually turned into a case study fit only for clinical psychology or a straitjacket. They are, as we might put it, 'pathologised': held up as someone who is actually crazy, rather than as an ordinary human who is essentially quite sane but has temporarily lost their self-possession in an extremely difficult situation.

On the other side of the equation, the person who remains calm is automatically cast – by their own imperturbable nature and subtle skills in public relations – as decent and reasonable. But we should bear in mind that it is, at least in theory, entirely possible to be cruel, dismissive, stubborn, harsh and wrong and to keep one's voice utterly steady. Just as one can, equally, be red-nosed, whimpering and incoherent and have a point.

We need to keep in mind a heroically generous attitude: Rage and histrionics can be the symptoms of a desperation that sets in when a hugely important, intimate truth is being blatantly ignored or denied, without the uncontrolled person being either evil or monstrous.

Obviously the method of delivery is drastically unhelpful; obviously it would always be better if we didn't start to cry. But it is not beyond understanding or, in theory at least, forgiveness if we were to do so. It's horrible and frightening to witness someone getting intensely worked up, but with the benefit of perspective, their inner condition calls for deep compassion rather than a lecture. We should remember that only someone who internally feels their life is in danger would end up in such a mess.

We should keep this in mind because sometimes it will be us who falls into a deranged state; we won't always be the aggrieved, cooler-headed party. We should all keep a little mental film of ourselves at our very worst moments from which we can replay brief highlights and so remember that, while we looked mad, our contortions were only the outer signs of an inner agony at being unable to make ourselves understood on a crucial point by the person we relied upon.

We can stay calm with almost everyone in our lives. If we lose our temper with our partners, it is (at best, in part) because we are so invested in them and our joint futures. We shouldn't invariably hold it against someone that they are behaving in a stricken way; it (probably) isn't a sign that they are mad or horrible. Rather, we should have the grace to remember that it is just that they love and depend on us very much.

VI. THE ESCALATION ARGUMENT

There are moments in a couple's life when what began as a simple conversation abruptly turns into a hugely vindictive row, because one party makes a move that – as their partner soon points out – is entirely out of proportion with the issue at hand.

A couple might be talking in a low-level way about some apparently insignificant matter: how they will get to the party that evening, whether it's time to invite their mother around again, if the correct pronunciation is o-re-ga-no or ore-ga-no. And then, with bewildering rapidity, a partner will level an accusation that seems wildly out of sync with the preceding dialogue. They may respond with untrammelled passion, 'Well, maybe I don't even want to go to the party. Why do our most precious moments always need the presence of a hundred witnesses? Why, in Italy last year, did you need to invite Mo, Dan, Ben and his sister too? What next, a camera so a thousand people can watch us making love – if we even did such a thing anymore?'

Or they might reply, with equal fury, 'You're always like this, aren't you? It's like last year at your dad's – every time I made a suggestion, you were onto me, showing me that I was wrong and implying that it's so hard for you to have to be with me. Why can't you just take my side on something for once?!'

At this point, the partner on the receiving end of these lines is liable to respond that there has been a gross violation of procedure, and that on this basis something very illegitimate has happened, which they have every right to be upset about and, henceforth, to focus the argument on. After all, the conversation was meant to be about whether to order a taxi for the party, not about what happened in Italy last year. Or it was meant to be about the best way to pronounce the Italian name of a particular herb, not the balance of power within the couple. It is deeply offensive that the topic should have swerved so violently and with so little warning. A new argument soon bubbles up about what it is right or fitting to argue about and how much warning should be given before a new and large point of contention is introduced.

We might term such disputes 'escalation arguments', where a discussion about topic X swiftly unleashes an only tenuously related but much larger accusation around Y, which the recipient dismisses as having been incorrectly introduced.

This kind of argument is symptomatic of a relationship in which emotional hygiene has not been followed: Areas of tension have not been correctly discussed, cleansed and 'flushed out', and so disappointments and ill feelings have been left to develop an energy, which has been waiting for too long to emerge. The person making the accelerated vindictive remark looks like they are being disproportionate and seems at fault for suddenly turning up the heat, but a dangerous wall of steam has been building up for which both parties are arguably responsible.

The person on the receiving end of the abrupt tirade is in a sense correct: They are right that it is extremely inconvenient and jarring to be confronted without decorum. They are also right that the point has come out too fast. But, more accurately regarded, the accuser is moving swiftly and directly to the core of an issue that should have been covered long ago. The escalated argument is signalling some unfinished business, which is interrupting the free and natural exchange of intimacy.

We should, when we can manage it, not hold it against our partner if they haven't followed correct conversational procedure. It should, in a sense, never be a bad time to bring up a big theme. More broadly, two lovers should regularly allow themselves to have a sequence of small arguments in order not to have to be surprised or swept away by enormous irregular ones.

VII. THE EVE-OF-JOURNEY ARGUMENT

Our partner is about to go away on a long trip for work. We're going to miss them a lot. We love them very much. We have only one more evening together. We're going to make sure it's a lovely one. Maybe we'll go out to the local Chinese restaurant or cook one of their favourite dishes and then watch a romantic comedy.

Except that's not how it turns out at all. Just as they're packing their bags, we get embroiled in a fight about their toothbrush, or what time we said we'd be ready to eat, or where the phone chargers are kept. The issue isn't really significant for us, but we feel – from a mysterious place – a willingness to get vindictive and unusually cross. We dial up the tension even though there's seemingly no imperative to do so; they are repeatedly conciliatory, but we deliberately drive things on in a negative direction until finally we are in a fight. The dinner gets called off, one of us slams a door and someone calls someone an idiot.

What could possibly lead us to behave in such a peculiar way at the very moment when we're about to say goodbye? Why spoil the remaining few hours? What's happening is that our yearning for love is meeting with a dark, intimate dread: that we are deeply dependent on a lover who we don't control, whose affection is out of our command and who is about to be taken away from us for a long time. We feel so vulnerable about their impending absence that, with a fruitless immaturity we probably aren't even fully aware of, we decide to reinvent what they mean to us in the first place. We choose to hate and therefore not miss them as an alternative to suffering from the intensity of our love for someone we can't possess entirely.

By squabbling, we are attempting some drastic surgery on our emotions: If only we can convince ourselves that we don't want their love, it may stop mattering so much to us that they won't be on the same continent to give it to us. If we reject them, their symbolic rejection of us, however unwilled (rationally we know that, that this is a trip they had no option but to go on), is cancelled out.

We would, of course, be wiser to endure their loss than attempt to stop it wounding us. We are due some suffering in any case; better that it should be over the real issue (that they'll be eight time zones away by tomorrow night) rather than its proxy (that they were a little impolite when asking if we'd seen their washbag).

VIII. THE ABSENTEE ARGUMENT

There are so many ways in which the world wounds us. At work, our manager repeatedly humiliates and belittles us; we hear of a party to which we were not invited; a better-looking, wealthier person snubs us at a conference; we develop a skill that turns out not to be much in demand in the world; some people we were at university with set up a hugely successful business.

Our hurt, humiliation and disappointments accumulate, but almost always we cannot possibly complain about these to anyone. Our managers would sack us if we told them how we felt; our acquaintances would be horrified by the depth of our insecurities; no one gives a damn about an admirable company that has hurt our feelings through its success. There is no way to take out our distress around geopolitics or economic history or the existential paradox that we are required to make decisions about our lives before we could possibly know what they will entail. We cannot rave at the cosmos or at the accidents of political power. We need, most of the time, simply to swallow our hurt politely and move on.

But there is one exception to this rule: We can rant and moan at a person who is more reliably kind to us than anyone else, a person whom we love more than any other, a blessed being who is waiting for us at home at the end of every new, gruelling day ...

Unfortunately, we don't necessarily always tell our partner that we are causing problems because we are

sad about things that have nothing to do with them –
we just create arguments to alleviate our distress; we
are mean to them because our boss didn't care, the
economy wasn't available for a chat and there was no
God to implore. We reroute all the humiliation and rage
that no one else had time for onto the shoulders of the
one person who cares most about our well-being. We
tell them that if only they were more supportive, less
intrusive, made more money, were less materialistic,
were more imaginative or less naive, less fussy or more
demanding, more dynamic or more relaxed, sexier or
less obsessed with sex, more intelligent or less wrapped
up in the world of books, more adventurous or more
settled ... then we could be happy, and our life would
be soothed and our errors redeemed. It is – as we imply
and occasionally even tell them – all their fault.

This is, of course, horrible and largely untrue. But

enfolded within our denunciations and absurd criticisms is a strangely loving homage. Behind our accusations is an inarticulate yet large compliment. We complain unfairly as a tribute to the extent of our love and the position the partner has taken in our lives.

We pick a fight with them over nothing much, but what we are in effect saying is, 'Save me, redeem me, make sense of my pain, love me even though I have failed.' The fact that we are blaming the partner in ridiculous ways is a heavily disguised but authentic mark of the trust we have in them. We must be civilised and grown up with everyone else, but with one person on the planet we can at points be maddeningly irrational, utterly demanding and horribly cross – not because they deserve it, but because so much has gone wrong, we are so tired and they are the one person who promises to understand and forgive us. No wonder we love them so much.

We are very alive to the idea that it's patronising to be thought of as younger than we are. We forget that it is also, at times, the greatest privilege for someone to look beyond our adult self in order to engage with – and forgive – the disappointed, furious, inarticulate and wounded child within.

IX. THE IDENTITY ARGUMENT

One of the great pleasures of relationships is the sense that another person knows us deeply. While we are either ignored or misrepresented by most of the world, in our unions we thrive from the gratifying sense that our identity has been accurately tracked, drawn and committed to memory. Our partner knows our favourite foods, our childhood traumas, our quirks around travel, our morning habits and our ambivalent feelings about certain friends.

But it is the extent and overall accuracy of this knowledge that can provoke sudden moments of claustrophobic irritation when our partners use their privileged overview of our character to level a claim about who we are that seems to reduce, caricature or limit us unduly, and is blind to our evolutions and aspirations for change.

'Don't be silly, you're not someone who ever enjoys holidays,' they might assert with the confidence and authority of someone who has shared our bed for close to a decade. Or, 'That's far too late for you, you're always asleep by ten.' Or, 'You've never liked dancing ...' Or, with real surprise when we come back from the library, 'But you don't even like books about politics ...' Or, to the attendant at the deli counter, 'No, no, they don't like pickles.'

The comments and the sure manner of their delivery reflect an experience of us built up over time through the patient work of love. But they can also prove wholly enraging. It feels as if the authority that the lover possesses has malignly been deployed to fix us into a role that no longer feels quite true. They are telling us who we are (the nicest thing in theory) but getting it rather wrong (about the worst thing in practice). Though a particular trait might admittedly have existed for many years, we may, beneath the surface, quietly be attempting to change. We are tentatively evolving. We no longer want to remain who we once were in every detail. We have original aspirations; we want to shed skins; we're trying to open ourselves up to different experiences. We want to give pickles a go.

And yet the partner has set themselves up as the jealous guardian of a self we no longer quite identify with. They insist that who we are now claiming to be must be false, pretentious, mean-spirited or an attempt to hoodwink others, all because it isn't who we have traditionally been.

Alongside physical development, we are engaged in a life-long process of psychological evolution, which is far harder to spot, to discuss and to give room to in others. Because we look more or less the same from the outside, those around us naturally assume that we must remain more or less the same on the inside too. Yet we are continually on the way to discovering new sides of ourselves; we're shedding allegiances, stretching ourselves in unfamiliar directions and clearing out irrelevant positions and enthusiasms. Perhaps we're gaining a new zone of confidence at work or we're getting more cautious and circumspect where we were once rather reckless. We might be discovering the beginnings of a new kind of passion for the arts where we used to be quite closed and judgemental, or perhaps we're firming up certain opinions around money or politics. We may be trying to relax more into our body or to outgrow an earlier prudish stance.

These changes may not yet be very clear even to us. There are no birthdays to mark them or public occasions to lend them weight; we can't easily explain them to our partner and may not be too sure how to make them sound plausible. We may also be slightly embarrassed because they seem to contradict previously well-defined attitudes which we know our partner was fond of or reassured by.

Yet the changes matter to us hugely. They are, in a way, the most important things going on in our inner lives right now and we are therefore acutely sensitive to anyone who might sweep away, or with a mocking laugh destroy, the tentative foundations of our future selves.

Children show us most clearly the passions unleashed when another person holds us too tightly to an earlier version of ourselves. At a party, a parent might explain of her child, 'Oh, he's five,' only to find the child approaching them a moment later and protesting in an intense, angry whisper, 'That's not true at all, I'm five and three quarters.' Giving due weight to our evolutions, be they bodily or emotional, can matter an awful lot.

That is why we can find ourselves in such intense arguments when a partner makes a remark that would have interested the person we used to be back in the spring, or they make a criticism which could have been very true of our outlook last Christmas, or they buy a jacket we would have loved three summers ago. What rankles is the static picture of who we are that's implied in what our partner has done – and that offends the part of us that associates intimacy with being given the space to evolve. Despite their love, our partner hasn't kept pace with our growth; they have failed to be sympathetic to the impulse for change; they are fixing us too tightly to a portrait that, though it was once satisfying, is no longer truly accurate.

The partner isn't being mean. Change is frightening, because the one evolution we are all terrified of is the kind that will take our beloved away from us. The reason we may get stubborn about a new love of pickles is that it stands as a harbinger of what might be a new love for another person.

The ideal solution would be to develop a view of the essential normality and unthreatening nature of growth. We will all, over a long-term relationship, evolve in a range of ways which have to undercut any settled claim by one person to 'know' another. What we grasp of our partner can only ever be partial and temporary, and we should not grow jealous or angry on that score alone. We are not like books, written once and shelved in a static library; we are like online texts, constantly edited from different directions.

True love requires us to allow our partner to become someone rather different than they were when we met them, and to welcome their evolutions rather than use the portrait we painted of them at the start as the fixed reference point from which any deviation has to be considered a disloyalty. The creature who emerges from the chrysalis is as likely to love us more intelligently and deeply as they are to want to fly away to someone new. We should use the phrase 'I don't understand you anymore' not as a despairing exclamation, but as a hopeful call to renew our sources of intimate insight.

It's common to accuse long-term relationships of being boring, but our tendency to evolve offers us a way out of the limitations of monogamy. We are – if we are correctly attuned to the phenomenon – only ever with the same person for a very short time. In truth, we cohabit with a constantly shifting array of people who just happen to have the same name and inhabit more or less the same body and lie next to us in similar ways in bed. Yet beyond these common points, such are their differences that they may really just as well be wholly new people. We can, in one relationship, without drama, enjoy an array of new lovers, embracing all the different versions of the one person we are with.

X. THE ARGUMENT OF NORMALITY

Being in a relationship, even a very good one, constantly requires us to defend our preferences and points of view against the possibility of a partner's objections. We can find ourselves having to argue about what time to go to bed, where to put the sofa, how often to have sex, what to do in a foreign city or what the best colour for a new car might be.

In previous eras, the sorts of justifications we wielded were far simpler. The person with more power would simply assert with haughty indifference, 'Because I say so,' or, 'Because I want it this way.' But now we live in a more civilised age focused on discussion, where only well-founded and articulated reasons are expected to swing a point.

Because we live in a democratic age too, one of the tools to which warring couples most often have to resort when attempting to justify their choices is majority opinion. That is, in the heat of a fight, we remind our opponent that what we want to do, think or feel is normal. We suggest that they should agree with us, not only or primarily because of what we happen to say, but because they'll find – once they stop to consider the matter with appropriate humility – that all right-thinking people agree with us too. Our position (on furniture arrangements, sexual routines or car colours) isn't mere idiosyncrasy. It is synonymous with that lodestar of contemporary ethics: 'normality'.

As we fight, we bolster our personal and therefore fragile opinion with the supposedly impregnable voice of the entire community: It is not simply that I – one solitary, easily overlooked person – find your attitude very displeasing. All reasonable people – in fact, an electoral majority of the world – are presently with me in condemning your ideas. You are – in your opinion on how to cook pasta, when to call your sister or the merit of a prize-winning novel – utterly alone.

In a pure sense, what is 'normal' shouldn't matter very much at all. What is widespread in our community is often wrong and what is currently considered odd might actually be quite wise. But however much we know this intellectually, we are profoundly social creatures; millions of years of evolution have shaped our brains so that we naturally give a great deal of weight to the opinions of those around us. In reality, it almost always feels emotionally crucial to try to retain the broad goodwill and acceptance of our community. So the claim to 'normality' (however approximately and unfairly it is made) touches on a sensitive spot in our minds, which is precisely why our partner invokes it so deftly.

Nevertheless, we should hold on to the counter-arguments. When it comes to personal life, we have no sound idea of what is normal, because we have no easy access to the intimate truths of others. We don't know what a normal amount of sex really is or how normal it is to cry, sleep in a different bed to our partner or dislike a partner's best friend. There are no reliable polls or witnesses. We are far more likely to build up an accurate picture of what is 'normal' by studying our own relationship than by taking our cues from TV shows or magazine articles.

Secondly, and more importantly, we should cease cynically lauding the idea of the normal when it suits us by acknowledging that almost everything that is beautiful and worth appreciating in our relationship is deeply un-normal. It's very un-normal that someone should find us attractive, should have agreed to go out with us, should put up with our antics, should have come up with such an endearing nickname for us that alludes to our favourite animal from childhood, should have bothered to spend some of their weekend sewing on buttons for us and should bother to listen to our anxieties late into the night. We are the beneficiaries of some extremely rare eventualities and it is the height of ingratitude to claim to be a friend of the normal when most of what is good in our lives is the result of awesomely miniscule odds. We should stop badgering our partners with phoney democratic arguments and admit to something far truer and possibly more effective in its honest vulnerability: that we would love for something to happen because, and only because, it would make us very happy if it did – and very upset if it didn't.

XI. THE PARENTAL RESEMBLANCE ARGUMENT

There is a move many of us make in the heat of an argument with our partner that is at once devastating, accurate and entirely uncalled for. In a particularly contemptuous, sly and yet gleeful tone, partners are inclined to announce, as if a rare truth was being unearthed, 'You're turning into your mother.'

The claim is apt to silence us because, however much we may have tried to develop our own independent characters, we can't help but harbour a deep and secret fear that we are prey to an unconscious psychological destiny. In one side of our brain, we are aware of a range of negative qualities that we observed in our parents which we sense are intermittently hinted at in our own personalities. And we are terrified.

We catch ourselves rehearsing opinions that once struck us as patently absurd or laughable. In moments of weakness, we find ourselves replaying just the same sarcastic or petty, vain or angry attitudes we once felt sure we would never want to emulate. The accusations of our partner hurt so much because they knock up against a genuine risk.

At the same time, the criticism is deeply underhand. Firstly, because even if we ourselves occasionally share an account of our parents' failings with our partners, the universal rules of filial loyalty mean that we – and only we – are ever allowed to bring these up again in an aggressive tone.

Secondly, the accusation is unfair because it is attempting to push us into denying something that is invariably partly correct. How could we not be a little like our parents, given the many years we spent around them, the untold genes we share with them and the malleability of the infant mind?

We should never get railroaded into protesting that we are unlike those who put us on the Earth; we should undercut the implicit charge by immediately, candidly admitting that we are, of course, very much like our parents, as they are akin to theirs. How could we be anything else! Why wouldn't we be! But in a twist to the normal argument, we should then remind our partners that we chose to be with them precisely in order to attenuate the risks of an unexamined parental destiny. It was and remains their solemn duty not to mock us for being like our parents, but to assist us with kindness to become a little less like them where it counts. By hectoring and accusing us, they aren't identifying a rare truth from which we hide away in shame; they are stating the obvious and then betraying the fundamental contract of adult love. Their task as our partner isn't to bully us into making confessions that we would have been ready to accept from the start; it's to help us to evolve away from the worst sides of people who have inevitably messed us up a little and yet whom we can't (of course, despite everything) stop loving inordinately.

XII. THE ARGUMENT FROM EXCESSIVE LOGIC

It seems odd at first to imagine that we might get angry, even maddened, by a partner because they were, in the course of a discussion, proving to be too reasonable and too logical. We are used to thinking highly of reason and logic. We are not normally enemies of evidence and rationality. How then could these ingredients become problematic in the course of love? But from close up, considered with sufficient imagination, our suspicion can make a lot of sense.

When we are in difficulties, what we may primarily be seeking from our partners is a sense that they understand what we are going through. We are not looking for answers (the problems may be too large for there to be any obvious ones) so much as comfort, reassurance and fellow feeling. In the circumstances, the deployment of an overly logical stance may come across not as an act of kindness, but as a species of disguised impatience.

Let's imagine someone who comes to their partner complaining of vertigo. The fear of heights is usually manifestly unreasonable: The balcony obviously isn't about to collapse; there's a strong iron balustrade between us and the abyss and the building has been repeatedly tested by experts. We may know all this intellectually, but it does nothing to reduce our sickening anxiety in practice. If a partner were patiently to begin to explain the laws of physics to us, we wouldn't be grateful; we would simply feel they had misunderstood us.

Much that troubles us has a structure akin to vertigo: our worry isn't exactly reasonable, but we're unsettled all the same. We can, for example, continue to feel guilty about letting down our parents, no matter how nice to them we've actually been. Or we can feel very worried about money, even if we're objectively economically quite safe. We can feel horrified by our own appearance, even though no one else judges our face or body harshly. Or we can be certain that we're failures who've messed up everything we've ever done, even if, in objective terms, we seem to be doing pretty well. We can obsess that we've forgotten to pack something, even though we've taken a lot of care and can, in any case, buy almost everything at the other end. Or we may feel that our life will fall apart if we have to make a short speech, even though thousands of people make quite bad speeches every day and their lives continue as normal.

When we recount our worries to our partner, we may receive a set of precisely delivered, unimpassioned, logical answers – we have been good to our parents, we have packed enough toothpaste, etc. – answers that are both entirely true and yet unhelpful as well, and so in their own way enraging. It feels as if the excessive logic of the other has led them to look down on our concerns. Because, reasonably speaking, we shouldn't have our worries, the implication is that we must be mad for having them.

The one putting forward the 'logical' point of view shouldn't be surprised by the angry response they receive. They are forgetting how weird and beyond the ordinary rules of reason all human minds can be, theirs included. The logic they are applying is really a species of brute common sense that refuses the insights of psychology. Of course our minds are prey to phantasms, illusions, projections and neurotic terrors. Of course we're afraid of many things that don't exist in the so-called real world. But such phenomena are not so much 'illogical' as deserving of the application of a deeper logic. Our sense of whether we're attractive or not isn't a reflection of what we actually look like; it follows a pattern that goes back to childhood and how loved we were made to feel by those we depended on. The fear of public speaking is bound up with long-standing shame and dread of others' judgement.

An excessively logical approach to fears discounts their origins and concentrates instead on why we shouldn't have them, which is maddening when we are in pain. It's not that we actually want our partner to stop being reasonable; we want them to apply their intelligence to the task of sensitive reassurance. We want them to enter into the weirder bits of our own experience by remembering their own. We want to be understood for being the mad animals we are, and then be comforted and consoled that it will (probably) all be OK anyway.

Then again, it could be that the application of excessive logic isn't an accident or form of stupidity. It might be an act of revenge. Perhaps the partner is giving brief logical answers to our worries because their efforts to be sympathetic towards us in the past have gone nowhere. Perhaps we have neglected their needs.

If two people were being properly 'logical' in the deepest sense of the word – that is, truly alive to all the complexities of emotional functioning – rather than squabbling around the question of 'Why are you being so rational when I'm in pain?', the person on the receiving end of the superficial logic should gently change the subject and ask, 'Is it possible I've hurt or neglected you?' That would be real logic.

XIII. THE ATTENTION-SEEKING ARGUMENT

One of the most obvious but in practice very hardest things to ask a partner, even one we name in our will and whose life is entirely entwined with ours, is, 'Do you still love me?' There would be so many reasons why they might not do so any more: We might have driven them to the limit with our admittedly, at points, rather challenging behaviour. We're not getting any younger. There are a lot of other people – especially at work and in the invisible parts of their life – who would have great things to offer them. It's hard to trust anyone, given what can happen. Furthermore, the signs aren't necessarily very good at the moment. They spend a lot of time on their phone. They're a bit distracted. Their thoughts seem elsewhere.

We powerfully long for reassurance, and at the same time what we would need to get this reassurance presents terrors all of its own. It would mean revealing the extent of our vulnerability and of the scale of their power to hurt us. It would mean having to admit how much of our life is in their hands and how deeply we depend on their good opinion for our psychological survival.

Sometimes the cost can feel just too high, especially if we grew up in families where we got little reassurance that another person would understand our needs. It seems better not to ask too directly. At the same time, their disengaged manner is unbearable as well. In the circumstances, we may find ourselves carrying out one of the strangest manoeuvres witnessed in relationships: We may seek to get their attention accompanied by their anger, as an alternative to securing their attention accompanied by their love. We choose to pay the lower price required to get signs that they remember we exist, rather than undertaking the far more arduous, rejection-threatening task of securing proof that they still love us.

So we wait until they are tired and fed up and launch a volley of accusations: 'You never do much around the house,' 'Your job doesn't pay enough,' 'You've become very dull.' Or, at dinner with friends, we loudly tell a story about something that happened during their parents' messy divorce.

What we are really trying to say is, 'I love you so much. I rely on you to give sense to my life.' But instead, we manage to work them up into a rage and ensure that they will say brutal things to us. Of course, their mind is fully trained on us, but it's far from the kind of attention we were seeking. We who crave their kindness, enthusiasm, compassion and constructive intelligence are on the receiving end of their frustration, wounded pride and self-protective anger.

We should have courage in our longings. We should build relationships in which it is natural, and therefore not too frightening, to seek and receive, on a regular basis, basic reassurance that we are wanted. We should make friends with our own extreme dependence and not see it as a sign of either weakness or evil. Furthermore, when we next find ourselves on the receiving end of some utterly unfair accusations or aggression from our partner, we should bear in mind that they have probably not turned monstrous; they are simply trying to secure a reminder that we care for them in the only way they know how: by driving us mad.

XIV. THE PARAPHRASE ARGUMENT

There are arguments that start with one person gently trying to explain a difficult situation to their partner: There's going to be an unfortunate clash of schedules around their birthday; the household budget has been overstretched; the car has received a dent; a friend has invited themselves to dinner ...

The partner will listen stony-faced for a while, and then interrupt with an extremely abrupt, or more accurately brutal, paraphrase of what they have just heard. 'If I'm getting this correctly,' they might summarise, 'you've just ruined the holiday.'

Person A: The long version	Person B: The paraphrase
'Because I was maybe a bit more ambitious in my sense of what income I'd be getting next month compared to the month before, I allowed myself to invest in some things that, with the benefit of hindsight, I'd perhaps not have gone for ...'	'We're bankrupt.'
'Jake told me that he might be around after seeing his sister, as he isn't going to go to the museum. And seeing as we have enough space here, and your mum won't come till tomorrow anyway, and there's a big lasagne in the fridge, I thought I might ask him to join us ...'	'Dinner is ruined.'
'We got close, we shared various things, but it never meant too much and it's nothing like what people might think. I never forgot what we had and have ...'	'You've slept with someone else and destroyed our marriage.'

It's easy to see why, in crucial areas of our lives, we crave the long and complicated explanations. They are the guardians of humanity and civilisation. They are rounded, sympathetic and kindly. Many great works of art are, in effect, lengthy explanations for actions which might, in less subtle hands, be cruelly paraphrased. A headline summary like 'Woman fucked around and spent all the money' can, when narrated by a complex genius, end up as Gustave Flaubert's masterpiece *Madame Bovary*. Great novels remind us that our motives, needs, anxieties and hopes are complicated and strange sounding, but told properly can win sympathy and understanding – and be revealed as deserving of the utmost dignity.

In the course of arguments, the one giving the long story is, in a sense, trying to be Flaubert. That is, they are trying to communicate a complicated, morally intricate, non-obvious set of truths. Why then, do their efforts tend to go so awry?

When a person in a couple has done something wrong or tricky, three things need to happen for the situation to start to be repaired. There should be:

1. an admission
2. an apology
3. an explanation

For the perpetrator, it is the third move that is the most compelling and significant. It's the explanation that will put their actions into context, that will stop them becoming a pariah in their own and the other's eyes and that will enable them to hold on to their humanity.

However, this is unlikely to be what is uppermost in

the minds of their partner. For them, it is the second point, the apology, that is most important and that will allow for repair, because it is a sign that the other has properly understood the difficulties they have caused and assumed due responsibility for them.

If the perpetrator keeps returning to the explanation and avoids the task of giving much by way of an apology, the recipient may – in frustration and hurt – seek revenge by zeroing in on the original admission, hammering home the deed until it is put in the crudest terms. It's not that they're unaware that there may be a host of subtle explanations to be heard; it's just that they are in no mood to hear them unless and until the perpetrator has taken appropriate responsibility.

Then again, the blame isn't on one side only. If the wounded party too readily suggests that they will be excessively vindictive, then the guilty party will have an understandable impetus to avoid overly candid admissions.

We bear, within couples, joint responsibility for facing up, with requisite gentleness, to one another's many misdeeds. We should have the chance to give the morally complicated explanations we deserve – once we have taken on the responsibility that is our due.

XV. THE ARGUMENT IN PARADISE

We're in paradise: a beachfront hotel on a tropical island, a charming cottage in a tranquil valley, a luxurious hotel in a historic city. Our spirits stand to be soothed by beauty and comfort. We've argued in the stressed, imperfect circumstances of home, but now we are free to be sweet, calm, thoughtful, tender and patient. We have come here quite deliberately to give ourselves a pleasant break and to restore our better feelings towards one another.

Yet it can be precisely in idyllic surroundings that we get especially irritated and frustrated with one another, and where some of our most explosive and bitter arguments may, ironically, be played out against a backdrop of quiet meadows and turquoise seas.

It seems especially aberrant and awful that this should happen when our cultural assumptions have no space for the strange shouting matches, brittle stand-offs and brutal confrontations that have followed us to paradise.

But there's a reasonable logic at work nevertheless: Because everything outward is particularly nice, the unhappy parts of our minds become more conspicuous. Our distresses weigh on us more heavily and announce themselves unusually loudly when bliss is demanded. Our high hopes of contentment make our frustrations with our partner (and secretly also with ourselves) even harder to accept. If only it weren't for them …

By contrast, it is sometimes our exposure to grim realities – to bleak stories of war, to tragedies and misfortune or to places where nature is hostile (a barren desert; a cold, craggy, storm-swept island) – that make our inner distress feel less important or pressing. We're more inclined to overlook our partner's annoying details in situations where having anyone at all feels like a privilege and where the entire human project seems fundamentally precarious and cursed.

Yet we should not compound our misery by declaring it illegitimate. We should mock our naive starting assumption that money and physical displacement could solve the problems that bedevil our scratchy partnerships, and accept that beautiful surroundings are only ever one ingredient – and certainly not the most powerful – to affect our lives. The capacity of great linen and succulent buffets to lift our mood is negligible as compared with the influence of honest communication or an opportunity to work through our resentments. Beautiful hotels teach us quiet lessons in the secondary importance of material goods.

But we should also skewer the fear that paradise must forever be marred by a few bust-ups. After the fight in the beachside bungalow or the flaming argument in the taverna, we will know that we have gloriously failed the challenge of living up to our surroundings and being a decent, mature person – and we will be all the better and more liberated for it. Of course we can't be totally happy or grown up for more than a few hours; this is simply how all humans are built (we just don't know enough about the lives of strangers to trust that we aren't the freakish exceptions). We haven't surrendered our right to be sad and vile just because we're paying a small fortune for a hotel room and there's a beautiful view out on the bay. The privileges of true paradise include the right to be, at points, just as miserable and fractious as we need to be.

XVI. THE SULK ARGUMENT

We're coming back from a lunch with friends, but something is wrong. Our partner on whom we depend so much has managed to offend us during the meal. It was the way they told an anecdote about our new shorts and seemed to laugh at our expense. Not that we're going to tell them. They've asked twice already if there is anything wrong, and we have firmly said, 'Nothing at all, I'm fine.'

With other people, we're always having to explain ourselves at length, and even when we do, they frequently struggle to catch our drift – but a true lover seems to get us almost immediately, even in the finer-grained aspects of our personalities. No sooner have we tried to explain, for example, our feelings towards autumn evenings, or that bit in a song we like when the violins start to rise, than they generously step in to say, 'I know, I know ...', seemingly ready to confirm our every sensation and idea.

This is a profoundly beautiful and exciting discovery, but it can give rise to hugely troubling dynamics in terms of the success of long-term relationships, for the view that a good lover must intuitively understand us is – over time – one of the most dangerous suppositions and is responsible for catastrophic outbreaks of sulking.

Sulking is a highly distinctive phenomenon within the psychology of arguments. Crucially, we don't just sulk with anyone. We reserve our sulks for people we believe should understand us but happen on a given occasion not to. We could explain what is wrong, of course, but if we did so, it would mean that they had failed to understand us intuitively and, therefore, that they are not worthy of love. A sulk is one of the odder gifts of love.

Our incensed background belief that a good lover should 'just know' explains why we sit quietly in the car all the way home, then disappear straight into the bathroom and bolt the door. When they ask again, 'Please tell me what's wrong,' we remain silent with our arms folded, for we implicitly believe that a true lover, someone really worthy of our affection, would naturally be able to discern how and why we got offended; would gaze through the bathroom panel, through our bodies and into the caverns of our burnt and pained souls.

Sulking has its touching side, evoking the enormous faith that we place in our partner's capacities to interpret us. But part of becoming an adult must be to believe that we cannot fairly continue to expect others to read our minds if we have not previously deigned to lay out their contents through the admittedly very cumbersome medium of words. Even the most intelligent, sensitive lover cannot be expected to continue to navigate around us without a lot of patiently articulated verbal indications of our desires and intentions.

We shouldn't get furious when our lovers don't guess right. Rather than bolting our mouths and retreating into the comforting silence of a sulk, we should have the courage – always – to try to explain.

XVII. THE CRUSH ARGUMENT

You are in a couple and are introduced to someone new at a conference. They look nice and you have a brief chat about the theme of the keynote speaker. But already, partly because of the slope of their neck and a lilt in their accent, you have reached an overwhelming conclusion. Or, you sit down in the train carriage and there, diagonally opposite you, is someone you cannot stop looking at for the rest of a journey across miles of darkening countryside. You know nothing concrete about them. You are going only by what their appearance suggests. You note that they have slipped a finger into a book, that they have a thin leather strap around their left wrist and that they are squinting a touch short-sightedly at the map above the door. And that is enough to convince you. Another day, coming out of the supermarket on your way home to your partner, amidst a throng of people, you catch sight of a face for no longer than eight seconds and yet here, too, you feel the same overwhelming certainty: You have a crush.

Crushes happen to some people often and to almost all of us sometimes. Airports, trains, streets, conferences – the dynamics of modern life are forever throwing us into fleeting contact with strangers, from among whom we pick out a few examples who seem to us not merely interesting, but more powerfully, the solution to our lives. Crushes could seem like negligible and absurd incidents, but they are also responsible for an enormous number of arguments and scratchy moments between couples.

When we return from the train ride or the conference, full of longing and desire, we are likely to be extremely dissatisfied with, or at least unpleasant around, our partner. In comparison with the divine being who has set our imagination in flight, all our partner's faults seem especially in evidence: their lack of tact, their clumsiness, their poor sense of humour, their simultaneously unpassionate yet sometimes nagging nature. No wonder we may be tempted to manufacture an argument to give expression to our sadness and frustration.

We blame our partner for our own spectacular bad luck in having ended up with such a mediocre love life, without realising that we are mistaking an asymmetry of knowledge for an asymmetry of quality; we are failing to see that it isn't the case that our partner is especially awful, but that we know them especially well. Our lovers are generally no worse than any charming stranger, but as they are familiar, their every failing has had a chance to be minutely charted.

The corrective to disproportionate knowledge is experience. We need to mine the secret reality of other people and so learn that, beneath their charms, they will almost invariably be essentially 'normal' in nature – that is, no worse yet no better than the candidates we already have in our lives.

The primary error of the crush lies in overlooking a central fact about people in general, not merely this or that example, but the species as a whole: that everyone has something very substantially wrong with them once their characters are fully known, something so wrong as to make an eventual mockery of the unlimited rapture unleashed by the crush. We can't yet know what the problems will be, but we can and should be certain that they are there, lurking somewhere behind the facade, waiting for time to unfurl them.

How can we be so sure? Because the facts of life have deformed all of our natures. No one among us has come through unscathed. There is too much to fear: mortality, loss, dependency, abandonment, ruin, humiliation, subjection.

We are, all of us, desperately fragile, ill-equipped to meet with the challenges to our mental integrity. We lack courage, preparation, confidence, intelligence. We don't have the right role models; we were (necessarily) imperfectly parented; we fight rather than explain, nag rather than teach; we fret instead of analysing our worries; we have a precarious sense of security; we can't understand either ourselves or others well enough;

we don't have an appetite for the truth and suffer a fatal weakness for flattering denials. The chances of a perfectly good human emerging from the perilous facts of life are non-existent. Our fears and our frailties play themselves out in a thousand ways; they can make us defensive or aggressive, grandiose or hesitant, clingy or avoidant – but we can be sure that they will make everyone much less than perfect and, at moments, extremely hard to live with.

The solution to the arguments that follow from a crush is to extrapolate from what we already know about people in general and apply it to those we don't yet know. The most plausible generalisation we can make about unknown people is that they are likely to be closer to what we've already experienced than they are to being completely – and bountifully – different. The cure for love is to get to know them better ... We should accept, with good grace and a touch of dark humour, that life simply gives us few opportunities to be totally content.

XVIII. THE LOST ITEM ARGUMENT

We must have put the keys on the ledge in the hall; we had to have done or how else would we have got in? And now they are missing. We have only minutes to find them or the day and possibly the week will be ruined. How could they have vanished in sly silence? Someone has maliciously moved them. They – the partner with whose life ours is intricately entwined – must have done so, without telling us, carelessly, with an utter disregard for our welfare.

It's not the first time. There was the missing pullover, the elusive file, the lost nail clippers ... The panic and anger that seizes us at such moments is beyond anything we can accept about ourselves when we are serene once more. We are stamping our feet. We are rasping incoherently. There is a plot against us. The missing item fundamentally mocks our claims to mastery; it turns the world into an absurdity. Everything ordered and predictable is undermined. We feel so certain and yet our certainty doesn't alter the absence one iota. Someone is mocking us. We know where we put the damn keys and yet the keys are still not there, even though they must be there, and yet they are not, and yet they must be, and yet they are not – and we look again and scream and look once more and still they are not there. We get on the phone to our partner at work and start to rant. It is as if malevolent goblins were following us around, deliberately making items vanish and slipping them into unusual pockets and folds in the universe.

'Where are they? Why did you move them? What are you trying to do to me?' It's madness, but it's also a tribute to the enormous role our lover plays in our lives that we do, at some level, hold them responsible for everything that happens to us, for good or ill. They took the keys; they hid the pullover; they know where the credit card must have gone. Our fury is a symptom of the continuation, deep into adult life, of the early fantasy of the child that their parents control the world and are capable of everything. It's they who make breakfast appear, who turn out the lights, who choreograph a holiday, who can make Bunny appear when he goes missing and who know how to find the lid to the favourite fat orange pen.

In blaming the lover, we're protecting a cherished belief: that they can fundamentally always change our fortunes; that they can make objects disappear and then reappear again at will; that they have supernatural powers; that they are in charge, that we are in love with someone who can pull the large levers of existence, that we're not helpless victims of fate.

It always feels strange when evidence subsequently emerges that it was really nothing of the sort. It is bewildering when later – maybe eight months later, our rage long spent – we stumble upon the missing item where we left it, in the pocket of the old coat or in a drawer in the kitchen between the aluminium roll and the elastic bands.

From the other side of the equation, we will know that someone else loves us when we start to encounter blame and rage not just for the things we have done, but for a much larger, more significant and almost flattering category: everything that saddens and frightens the one we love.

XIX. THE ARGUMENT FROM GUILT

We've been wasting all day on the Internet. One diversionary click turned into a thousand. It started with a news site and ended up in some very silly or very vile (or both) places. We've seen stuff we should never have seen; we've wasted our time outrageously; we've squandered our talents and betrayed the trust of those (from our school teachers to our parents, our children to our lover) who had the imagination to develop faith in us; we've thoroughly disgraced ourselves. And now our partner is home, full of bustle, purposefulness and the smell of the outdoors, with some shopping for dinner and a deep excitement at seeing us.

We aren't possibly in any position to meet such a set of expectations, but nor are we geared to explain how and why we aren't either. We're not going to tell them how time flew between 9 a.m. and now, just before 7 p.m. We won't tell them what we saw and how we couldn't bring ourselves to stop. Our societies talk a lot about the burdens of being loved too little – everyone has sympathy for that – but we collectively fail to talk enough about the pressures of being loved too much, when the veneration doesn't tally with our sense of ourselves, when we're feeling like wretches inside but the lover continues to hold a benevolent and kindly image of us.

Rather than just saying we don't deserve their love, we try to show that we couldn't possibly be worthy of kindness or forgiveness. We pick a major fight. We say something extremely mean. We insult their bottom or their anecdotes. We say that perhaps we won't go on the holiday we've jointly planned, or that their mother is boring.

And then they start to hate us and tell us we're awful, and while we protest, we feel at some level very pleased that the outer judgement now matches the inner sentiment of sin. We don't directly tell them, but we are grateful to them for sparing us the asphyxiating embrace of unearned affection. The drama (for this is what we have ensured it's become) helps us to relocate an equilibrium; it functions as a bracing penance.

Their loathing helps us to feel at home with ourselves once more. It accords so much better with who we are. We know we deserve punishment a good deal more than we might deserve a tender embrace.

Like a religious penitent, we try to win back their good grace. We make them tea, we do the laundry, we go out in the rain on a largely superfluous errand – what counts is that we suffer, and we must, for that is the lot of criminals and lowlifes.

Against the backdrop of ill temper and sourness, we slowly rebuild our sense of ourselves, apologise sincerely and, after many chores, recover a sense that we might have some potential. We vow to ourselves that tomorrow we will start afresh, with a cleaner soul, and try at last to be the sort of person who can meet the expectations bestowed on us by love.

XX. THE NO-SEX ARGUMENT

The no-sex argument could, on the surface, be an argument about almost anything: what time to leave for the airport, who forgot to post the tax form, where to send the children to school. But in reality, in disguise, unmentioned and unmentionable, it is typically the very same argument: the no-sex argument, the single greatest argument that ever afflicts committed couples, the argument which has powered more furious oblique exchanges among lovers than any other, the argument that, right now, explains why one person is angrily refusing to speak to another over a bowl of udon noodles in a restaurant in downtown Yokohama, and another is screaming in an apartment on an upper floor of a block in the suburbs of Belo Horizonte; why a child has acquired a step-parent and a person is crying over a bottle or in their therapist's office.

The real injury – you have ceased to want me and I can no longer bear myself or you – can't be mentioned because it cuts us too deep; it threatens too much of our dignity; it is bigger than we are. Late at night, in the darkness, time after time, our hand has moved towards theirs, tried to coax theirs into a caress and was turned down. They held our fingers limply for a moment and then, as if we were the monster we now take ourselves to be, curled away from us and disappeared into the warren of sleep. We have stopped trying now. It may happen once in a blue moon, a few times a year, but we understand the score well enough: We are not wanted. We feel like outcasts, the only ones to be rejected in this way, the victims of a rare disease, nursing an emotional injury far too shaming to mention to others, let alone ourselves – the only ones not be having sex in a happy, sex-filled world.

Our anger aggravates our injury and traps us in cycles of hostility. Perhaps they don't want us in the night because we have been so vile in the day. But so long as our hand goes unwanted, we can never muster the courage to be anything but vindictive in their presence. It hurts more than being single, when at least the neglect was to be expected. This is a sentence without end. We can neither complain nor let the issue go. We feel compelled to fight by proxy about anything we can lay our hands on – the washing powder and the walk to the park, the money for the dentist and the course of the nation's politics – all because we so badly need to be held and to hold, to penetrate or to be penetrated.

It is, in a sense, deeply strange, even silly, that so much should hang on this issue – that the future of families, the fate of children, the division of assets, the survival of a friendship group should depend on the right sort of frottage of a few centimetres of our lower limbs. It's the tiniest thing and at the same time the very largest.

The absence of sex matters so much because sex itself is the supreme conciliator and salve of all conflict, ill feeling, loneliness and disinterest. It is almost impossible to make love and be sad, indifferent or bitter. Furious, perhaps, in a passionate and ardent way, but not – almost always – truly elsewhere or beset by a major grievance. The act forces presence, vulnerability, honesty, tenderness, release. It matters inordinately because it is the ultimate proof that everything is, despite everything, still OK.

As ever, so much would change if only we could be helped to find the words, if we could fight our way past our shame, if we didn't have to feel so alone (this should be proof enough that we aren't), if we could point to the problem without fury, without humiliation, without defensiveness, if we could simply name our desperation without becoming desperate, if the one who didn't want it could explain in terms that made sense and were bearable, and the one who felt cast aside could explain without giving way to vindictiveness or despair.

We would ideally, alongside physics and geography, learn the basics of all this in our last year at high school; learn how to spot and assuage the no-sex argument with an in-depth course and regular refreshers throughout our lives. It is the paradigm of all arguments. Those who can get over it can surmount pretty much any dispute; those who cannot must squabble to the grave.

Were our species to learn how to do this, the world would be suddenly and decisively calmer; there would be infinitely fewer fights, alcoholic outbursts, divorces, affairs, rages, denunciations, recriminations, civil wars, armed conflicts and nuclear conflagrations. At the first signs of a no-sex argument, couples would know how carefully to locate the words that would address their sorrows. There would not always be an answer, but there would always be the right sort of conversation.

TOWARDS LESS BITTER ARGUMENTS

There are couples that seem never to argue. Their relationships are marked by enormous outward politeness: They say thank you a lot; they make each other cups of tea; they can look rather horrified when there's a mention of a squabble in someone else's life. It's understandable if they're privately a little pleased with themselves.

But surface harmony isn't, in reality, any reliable sign of health in love because it's impossible to try to merge two lives without regularly encountering deep sources of incompatibility. A lack of arguments is more likely to be a sign that we have given up caring than a superhuman achievement of maturity.

The goal isn't, therefore, to do away with arguments, but to find our way towards their more fruitful variety. We need to learn to argue well, rather than not to argue at all.

What, then, are some of the ideas that might help us have better arguments?

1. The single greatest idea that can help us to argue more constructively is to remind ourselves publicly that we are – both of us – by nature deeply imperfect and at points quite plainly mad. The enemy of mature arguments is self-righteousness: the sense that we might be beyond fault and that our partner must be either wicked for making a mistake or unfairly critical

in alleging that we have been guilty of one. It is of immense benefit if relationships can be conducted under the assumed truth that both participants are idiotic, mentally wobbly, quite flawed in manifold ways and constantly in need of forgiveness. It's an implicit faith in our own perfection that turns us into monsters.

2. People concede points not when they're aggressively told they're wrong but when they feel loved. We get stubborn and withhold the truth when we're scared and suspect that the person challenging us hates us, means us harm, can never forgive us – and is perhaps about to leave us. It is indispensable to preface every criticism with an assurance of our ongoing love.

3. People change very slowly, and seldom when they are harassed into doing so. We must strive not to be desperate for change. We must make our peace with

the idea that they won't evolve as we would wish on the timescale that would suit us; we should be rather pessimistic about human nature in order to encounter one or two grounds for hope.

4. We shouldn't aggravate our frustration by a sense that we have been uniquely cursed in ending up in this relationship. Of course they are annoying. Everyone in the world would be equally tricky to deal with at times and often probably a lot worse. The specifics of why we're in an irritating dispute may be local, but that we are in one is a universal destiny. We should laugh darkly at the human tragedy.

5. Our partner is only ever frightened, worried and not thinking straight, rather than bad. Just like us, they carry a lot of emotional baggage; they have been shaped by their complex and, at moments, very troubled history.

Much of what they do isn't directly about us but is a way of coping with difficulties that came into their life long before we met them.

6. Choose the moment. We can be under the illusion that arguing is an exchange of intellectual ideas, but it's largely a process reliant on our emotions and it is decisively influenced by such easily overlooked matters as how much sleep we've had, how much we've drunk and what time it is. As a general rule, wait until tomorrow.

7. Don't let the relationship die from misplaced 'politeness' or embarrassment. Dare to name the problem, however shocking it sounds. As long as it's been carefully wrapped in layers of love, the truth is normally bearable to those who care for us.

8. It doesn't matter if we're right. We must be prepared to forego all the pleasures of proving a point. We're not trying to 'win' but to live as happily as possible with another person who is, in the end, on our side and our best friend.

Despite this, we will still have furious rows, of course. We will call each other the worst things, slam doors and cry. It's hugely normal. The capacity to be horrible to a partner is even a strange – though genuine – feature of love. A relationship has to include the madder, more unreasonable parts of our nature; if we are only ever polite, it's because we have not been made to feel safe. A row may have to be the turbulent passage towards the kind of deeper reconciliation we long for. It can be important to say some wild and hurtful things to halt a drift apart. By foregrounding for a while the most extreme points of conflict, we set up the conditions for reconnecting with larger areas of closeness. We now remember that, despite an evening squabbling like the frightened, foolish, barely semi-rational idiots we are, we love them deeply nevertheless and will strive with all our will (and the help of the odd book like this) to argue a little more sensibly next time.

THE LOVE SERIES

There is no more joyful or troublesome area of our lives than love. From adolescence onwards, it is rare to go for any sustained length of time without some sort of fascinating or devilish new problem emerging around relationships.

The Love Series by The School of Life aims to be like an ideal friend around the dilemmas of the heart. Each title zeroes in on one of the central issues we're liable to confront – from dating to heartbreak, from affairs to arguments. What unites the books is their combination of psychological insight, humanity and warmth: They lend us the advice and comfort we need to find the happiness we deserve.